THE ⚜ TIMES

TEST YO
CREATIV
THINKING

Lloyd King

KOGAN
PAGE

First published in Great Britain in 2003

Kogan Page Limited
120 Pentonville Road
London N1 9JN
United Kingdom
www.kogan-page.co.uk

British Library Cataloguing in Publication Data

A CIP record for this book is available from the British Library.

ISBN 0 7494 4004 X

Typeset by Saxon Graphics Ltd, Derby
Printed and bound in Great Britain by Biddles Ltd, Guildford and King's Lynn
www.biddles.co.uk

Contents

Introduction

Creative thinking is a magical ability, which can both enhance our lives on a personal level and catapult us into another reality or way of seeing the world. Until quite recent times it was still widely believed to be some sort of supernatural gift bestowed on only a few tortured artists, musicians and scientists. Of course today we now know that this is just a myth and that almost everyone is born with the potential to be creative. But whether it blooms, withers or remains dormant is still very much dependent on luck. To a large degree this is due to an imbalance in our educational systems, which tend to target critical thinking skills almost to the exclusion of creative thinking ones. The unfortunate outcome of this is that our creative potential remains almost entirely forgotten and untapped. Albert Einstein had this to say about the problem: 'The intuitive mind is a sacred gift and the rational mind is a faithful servant. We have created a society that honours the servant and has forgotten the gift.' Such an imbalance defies logic. As lateral thinking expert Edward de Bono pointed out, 'Without creativity, there would be no progress, and we would be forever repeating the same patterns.' The good news is that you can learn to reawaken your creativity, shake off your old thought patterns and start creating some new ones.

The area of the brain most commonly associated with creative thinking is the right hemisphere, which, as well as being the visual, holistic and intuitive side, is also home to the imagination. While it is undoubtedly a major protagonist in the creative process, other areas of the brain also play a significant part in what is really a 'global' or whole-brain process. For example, the more critical, linear and logical left hemisphere of the brain supplies the essential raw data for the right hemisphere to synthesize. It does this via the corpus callosum, a bundle of more than 200 million nerve fibres, which forms a bridge between the two cerebral hemispheres and allows them to communicate. In addition, the left hemisphere is responsible for the analysis and the evaluation of any ideas, insights or solutions generated by the right hemisphere.

Creative thinking is all about having ideas. The ultimate purpose is to bring into existence something startlingly original, culturally acceptable and useful too. To think creatively you also need to be creative in the way that you think. This means thinking divergently, laterally, fuzzily, overinclusively, provocatively, synesthetically, 'outside the box' and, as has already been mentioned, analytically too. It requires breaking out of familiar patterns of thought, being flexible, and coming up with new and unusual associations and possibilities between seemingly unrelated ideas and things. In addition, it means being able to tolerate ambiguity, being able to see things from many different angles at the same time, and being able to change strategies at the drop of a hat in order to avoid getting 'stuck'. In his book *No Ordinary Genius* about the Nobel Prize-winning physicist Richard Feynman, Marvin Minsky says of him, 'He was so "unstuck" and if something didn't work he would look at it in another way. He had so many different good ways. He would do something in ten minutes that might take the average physicist a year.'

A characteristic of creative thinkers is that they like to do things in novel and unusual ways. They are not afraid to take risks and try new ideas, even though they might be wrong and appear foolish. As the poet Johann Wolfgang von Goethe said, 'Daring ideas are like chessmen moved forward; they may be beaten, but they may start a winning game.'

They also possess something called entelechy, which is the vital force that pushes you to make the most of your potential and work towards a specific goal. According to psychologist Howard Gruber, 'the creative person cannot simply be driven, he (or she) must be drawn to his work by visions, hopes, joy of discovery, love of truth, and sensuous pleasure in the creative activity itself.' Being iconoclastic and having a disregard for routine and order, creative thinkers can tend to live chaotically. But this is not necessarily a bad thing. In fact A A Milne, the author of *Winnie The Pooh*, said, 'One of the advantages of being disorderly is that one is constantly making exciting discoveries.'

Creative individuals have a childlike sense of playfulness and wonder as well as an unquenchable zest for life. It is as if they never grew up. Consequently, they tend not to take things too seriously and so retain their natural spontaneity. Also, they do not become too complacent or allow their thought processes to become predictable and stuck in a rut. After all, humans are not trams or trains confined to tramlines or railway lines and should be free to move in any direction they please. In some ways to be a creative thinker you must become a sort of ghost so that you are no longer confined by walls and can walk through them as though they do not exist.

More often than not creative thinking involves recombining and expanding existing ideas to generate new theories and concepts. Isaac Newton famously acknowledged this process when he said, 'If I have seen a little farther than others, it is because I have stood on the shoulders of giants.' The artist Vincent Van Gogh used what he had learnt from the new ideas of the impressionist artists like Monet and neo-impressionists like Georges Seurat to forge his own highly original and expressive style. Pablo Picasso too was greatly influenced by the ideas and work of other artists and art movements. He was particularly inspired by the post-impressionist Paul Cezanne and by tribal art. Their combined influence eventually led him and Georges Braque to invent Cubism with its radical simultaneous depiction of objects from multiple viewpoints.

Sometimes when the conscious mind cannot resolve a problem the subconscious mind continues to work away at it behind the scenes. Then, after a period of incubation, a solution unexpectedly bubbles to the surface. This happened to the German poet Rainer Maria Rilke. He was working on a long poem called the *Duino Elegies* when he fell into a deep depression that lasted for 10 years. Incredibly, when it did finally lift, he managed to complete this poem and also write the entire *Sonnets to Orpheus*, a total of 1,200 lines, almost without revision in just 18 days. Such an apparently effortless burst of creativity is known as a period of 'flow'. When people are in this trance-like state they may describe themselves as being 'in the zone' or 'on a roll'. There is an altered perception of time, a sharpening of the senses, and ideas just seem to pour out. Perhaps the most famous example of this phenomenon is Mozart. He said:

> When I am, as it were, completely myself, entirely alone, and of good cheer – say, travelling in a carriage, or walking after a good meal, or during the night when I cannot sleep; it is on such occasions that ideas flow best and most abundantly. Whence and how they come, I know not; nor can I force them.... Nor do I hear in my imagination the parts successively but I hear them, as it were, all at once.... The committing to paper is done quickly enough, for everything is already finished; and it rarely differs on paper from what it was in my imagination.

Ideas sometimes occur unexpectedly in a flash of inspiration called an 'Aha!' or 'Eureka!' moment. In Zen Buddhism such a state of sudden intuitive enlightenment is known as 'satori'. This is how the idea for Harry Potter came to author J K Rowling. She was taking a long train journey from Manchester to London in England and the idea for Harry just fell into her head. Another recent example is Trevor Bayliss's clockwork radio. This seemingly incongruous idea suddenly 'hit' him after he had been watching a television programme about the alarming spread of AIDS in Africa. The programme had mentioned the problem of providing sex education in isolated regions without electrical power. In an instant he realized that a wind-up radio could help to solve the problem. Straight away he went into his workshop and began working on the idea.

Similarly, the idea for 'liquid paper' came out of the blue. As a secretary Bette Graham found that mistakes made using the new electric typewriter ribbons could not be erased. Being an amateur artist, it suddenly occurred to her that, if artists can simply paint over their mistakes on canvas to hide them, why couldn't typists do the same? To test out her idea, she put some tempera water-based paint of the same colour as the paper she used in a bottle and took it to work. Using one of her paintbrushes, she began painting over her typing mistakes. It worked. Her boss didn't even notice.

Dreams are a great source of inspiration for ideas, and many artists, writers and musicians have claimed that their best ones came to them while they were asleep. For instance, the melody for the classic Beatles' song *Yesterday*, one of the most popular songs ever written, came to Paul McCartney in a dream. Apparently, it seemed so beautiful and vivid that for a while he was not sure that it was original.

A bizarre dream about a snake biting its tail led the chemist Friedrich August Kekulé to discover the ring structure of benzene. Here is his account of the experience:

I turned my chair to the fire and dozed. Again the atoms were flitting before my eyes. This time the smaller groups kept modestly in the background. My mental eye, rendered more acute by repeated visions of this kind, could now distinguish larger structures, of manifold conformation; long rows, sometimes more closely fitted together; all twining and twisting in snakelike motion. But look! What was that? One of the snakes had seized hold of its own tail, and the form whirled mockingly before my eyes. As if by a flash of lightning, I awoke.

Daydreaming too is very important in the creative process because it allows you to experience the deeper, intuitive processes of the mind. It happens when we go 'inside' ourselves and enter what is known as an 'alpha state', which is when we are relaxed, 'unfocused' and our alpha brainwave levels are low. For this reason the period just before we go to sleep is especially conducive to this type of thinking. If you have ever driven a car and been unable to remember part of the journey, this would have been because you experienced an 'alpha state'. The writer Mary Shelley famously conceived her nightmarish horror tale *Frankenstein* as she lay half-awake late at night. To access this state, start breathing deeply and slowly, making sure you hold your breath briefly between breaths. This will oxygenate your brain, promote alpha brainwaves and relax your body and mind so that you enter a state of calmness and heightened awareness. Immersing yourself in a relaxing bath is also a very good way to induce this state. It may be no coincidence, therefore, that Archimedes' famous 'Eureka!' moment happened while he was taking a bath.

There are many simple things you can do to help improve your creative thinking ability. For example, you could try listening to classical music. Studies have found that the corpus callosum of musicians is thicker and more developed than in non-musicians, suggesting that listening to music, particularly classical, enlarges neural pathways and stimulates learning and creativity. Furthermore, scientific research has shown that the brain does not stop rewiring and adapting itself after the age of five, as was once believed, but remains plastic and malleable throughout life. It is actually very similar to a muscle in that the more it is used, the more it grows and the stronger it becomes. Also, the more you challenge your brain, the more neural pathways are forged and the more you can understand the world around you. Neurologists call this 'use-dependent plasticity'. So even in old age there is considerable potential for cognitive improvement. Interestingly, Charles Darwin wrote in his autobiography, 'If I had to live my life again I would have made a rule to read some poetry and listen to some music at least once a week; for perhaps the parts of my brain now atrophied could thus have been kept active through use.' Here is a list of suggestions to help you get started. You might like to try using your creativity to come up with some ideas of your own.

- Take regular physical exercise.
- Eat a varied and balanced diet.
- Practise relaxation and meditation techniques.
- Improve your self-confidence.
- Keep a journal, doodle and write poems, short stories and songs.
- Read imaginative fiction.
- Practise thinking of alternative uses for everyday objects.
- Practise finding similarities between dissimilar things.
- Take up artistic pursuits like painting or sculpting.
- Visit inspirational places.
- Take up activities you wouldn't normally think of doing.
- Try being more spontaneous and outgoing.
- Watch comedy and try developing your own particular style of humour.

- Listen to classical music.
- Regularly look for ways to break out of your comfort zone.
- Do everyday things and routines in a different way.
- Make new friends and expand your social circle.
- Think of yourself as a creative person.
- Think of creativity as a way of life.
- Model yourself on a famous creative person you admire.
- Develop a rebellious streak.
- Get into the habit of what-if-ing.
- Don't watch too much television.
- Allow yourself to daydream.
- Don't be afraid to be wrong or make mistakes.
- Don't be too hasty in making judgements.
- Be curious about everything.

Tackling lateral puzzles is also a great way to stretch and improve your creative thinking skills. This book contains two sections of puzzles, one easy and the other hard. After each of these sections there is a fun test for you to take so that you can see whether or not your creative thinking ability has improved. But before diving straight into the first section of problems, you may find it helpful to try the two following warm-up puzzles to put you in the right frame of mind. As with the rest of the puzzles in this book, though, don't be too eager to look up the answers. If you really want to enjoy the 'Aha!' moments and learn something about creative thinking, be sure to give your subconscious enough incubation time to come up with the solutions before giving up. For while you may find that you are completely clueless one moment, the next you may just 'get it'. OK now: in the words of Mrs Doubtfire, played by the very creative actor and comedian, Robin Williams, 'Go pump some neurons.'

1. **Canine conundrum**

   Move two matches so that this dog sounds like a dog.

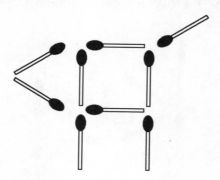

2. **Plus four**

   Add four more toothpicks to make this equation correct.

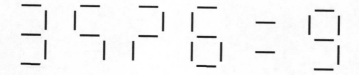

Answers

1. Rearrange the two matches to form K9, which sounds like canine.

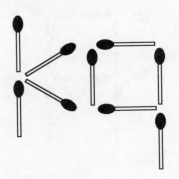

2.

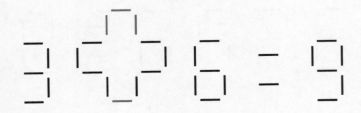

PART 1

Easy puzzles

1. **Small time**

One lunchtime grandpa peered up at this clock from his armchair. Due to his short-sightedness, though, he couldn't see if the minute hand was pointing to the fourth or fifth minute division line. He therefore asked grandma, who was seated much nearer the clock, which line it was pointing to. 'Well,' she replied, 'it is pointing to one of those minute division lines.' Surprisingly, grandpa then knew that it was 4 minutes past 12. How did he know?

2. ✓ **Seconds out**
   Which is the odd one out?

   > A mire
   > A minister
   > A cove
   > A vent
   > A verse

3. **Filling in time**
   Can you fill in the rest of the letters?

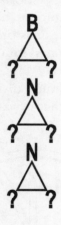

4. ✓ **A three letter problem**

Dr Watson and Sherlock Holmes are in a cab on their way to investigate another mystery when Holmes turns to Watson, who is about to doze off, and asks him this simple question:

> Which three consecutive letters of the alphabet can be placed in front of the four letters TARY in alphabetical order to spell a simple English word?

Watson doesn't know. Do you?

5. ✓ **Taxi**

Which taxi below is out of order?

A   B   C

6. Prediction

Cindy, a graphic artist, is drawing a picture of a playing card and is about to add the number in the top left-hand corner. However, before she does, can you predict how many hearts there will be on the completed card?

7. The saucy sorcerer

One day a saucy sorcerer winks at a witch. She immediately pays him back by turning him into a toad. Can you take away six of the seven shapes below to leave a sort of toad?

8. ✓ **Just what the doctor ordered**

Rearrange the following to create a 15-letter word.

SUE TICKLES FARMER

9. **Secret plot**

What do you call a plot of land that is 3 by 18 by 15ft?

10. **Try it**

To open a security door you must enter the specific five-letter password indicated below by pressing the buttons. What word should you 'try'?

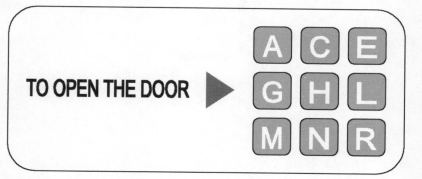

TO OPEN THE DOOR ▶
A C E
G H L
M N R

11. Missing letters

What are the missing letters?

  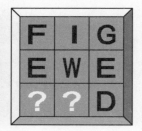

12. ✓ Square number

Move one match to leave a different square number.

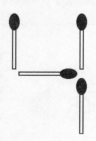

13. Rhyme time

What letter should replace the question mark?

1p, 2p, 3p, 4,
5p, 6p, 7p?.

14. Lunchtime

What do the two hands indicate that Jemima eats for lunch at 12:55 on this clock: 2 avocados, 1 banana, 2 mushrooms, 10 French fries or 4 tomatoes?

15. Playing with matches

Rearrange one match in this seven-letter word to leave seven of the same letter.

16. Cold fusion

Which is the missing letter: B, J, K, P, V, or Y?

N - W M O N S

17. Odd one out
Which is the odd word out and why?

ABOMINABLE
MOON
APIARY
BAMBOO
BUBBLE

18. Letter wheel
Fill in the dashes to leave an 11-letter word going clockwise.

19. Nom de plume
By what name is Anton Fepuni the well-known writer better known? (8 and 3 letters).

20. Treasure Island

What gems may be found on an island on this map?

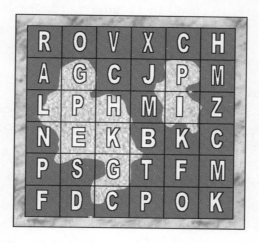

21. Twenty digits

Can you complete this set of 20 digits?

_I_9__5, ____b5 ___ _0_5

22. Make it count

Can you correctly fill in the two missing crosses in the last box?

23. **Inside out**

    Two familiar English words can be placed in the brackets below to create an 11-letter word. These are?

    $$P(???)N(?????)S$$

24. **Not to scale**

    Jenny weighs something with a set of scales. It weighs 5 kilograms. Can you figure out what it is and insert the missing letters below?

    $$? A ? I ? U ?$$

25. **Friends**

    Jeff, who lives in Manhattan, receives this message from his pal, Katrina:

    Jeff,

    See you on Friday at X.

    Katrina

    Where in Manhattan should he meet her?

26. **Chinese takeaway**

Melissa goes into a Chinese takeaway with exactly £21, all in one-pound coins. She buys a meal costing two pounds and leaves with twenty–one pound coins. How come?

27. **Time rationale**

A train departs from London at 5:10 and arrives at Birmingham one hour and fifty-five minutes later at 10:12. What is the explanation?

28. **Odd one out**

Which is the odd one out?

Au, Fe, He, Ma, Se, No

29. **Animal, vegetable or mineral**

If it is a river in India and an insect in Cuba, what is it in Japan: an animal, a vegetable or a mineral?

30. Come to some arrangement

Take away the two matchsticks indicated by the arrows and then rearrange the two remaining matchsticks to leave a capital H.

31. Island

In which lake or ocean is the little island pictured below found?

32. **Stately home**

Ted and Erica are lying on either side of a broken sofa in their uncle's stately home. What is his name (3 letters)?

33. **Surreal**

A magician recently asked me a simple, but bizarre sounding question: 'How do you make a matchstick out of an orange?' I didn't know. Do you?

34. **Magic circle**

Can you fill in the missing letters?

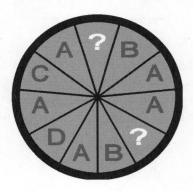

35. Word search

What is the longest English word that can be found in this grid by going from square to square in any direction and by using each letter any number of times? Incidentally, the answer is not withstanding.

36. Horseplay

This horse, which is facing to the left, is made up of four toothpicks and a match. Can you rearrange the match to leave it facing in the opposite direction?

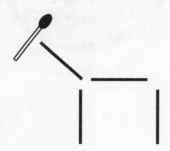

37. It just doesn't add up

How can you write down one thousand and forty-nine and then add fifty-one on to get a million?

38. Plane and simple

A jumbo jet takes off from Heathrow airport, London, at half two in the afternoon and lands at John F Kennedy, New York, which is five hours behind, seven hours later at 3 pm local time. How is this possible?

39. State the obvious

Which US state is 0°?

40. Correct time

How can you tell that this clock is both working and correct?

41. **Line M up**

Add two straight lines to this letter M, both longer than those below, to leave a different letter.

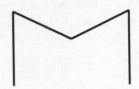

42. **A bit of a hoot!**

Find eight other ways of arranging the top cube, which has just the two letters shown on its sides, to create an owl. It is fairly easy to find seven, but the eighth is a little more tricky.

43. Starting block

What five-letter word goes in front of the following words?

> _MAN
> _SUIT
> _SHIP
> _CRAFT
> _LAB

44. On the make

A car goes from A to Y, then back to A. What make of car is it?

45. Group therapy

Some matchsticks are arranged in two groups, A and B. Amazingly, it is possible to move just one matchstick from group A to group B and yet leave the same number of matchsticks in each group. Can you see how it can be done?

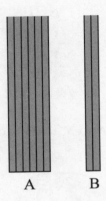

A   B

46. ✓ False start

What three-letter word completes the first word and starts the second one?

$$DON(\_\_\_)CAR$$

47. **Make a meal of it**

What's for supper on this dining table?

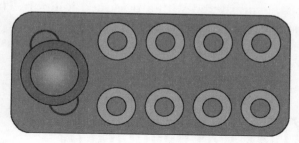

48. **3D puzzle**

Rotate two of these lettered discs to leave a seven-letter word.

49. Who doesn't love ya, baby?

At a meeting of four famous detectives in Los Angeles Kojak is murdered with a poisoned lollipop. The three suspects are Cannon, Columbo and Ironside. During the ensuing investigation the LAPD receive this anonymous tip-off:

Kojak was murdered by ___.

Which one of the three detectives does it implicate?

50. Novelty item

Find the next figure in this sequence.

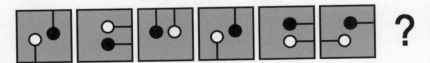

Choose from:

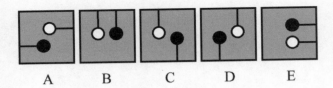

A   B   C   D   E

51. Put on the spot

Can you add 'O' to these five letters to leave a familiar word?

52. Marking time

Here are Kenny's answers to a quiz. Can you finish marking them and then find out how many he got right?

1. COARSE ✓
2. ACROSS ✓
3. VICTORIA ✗
4. ARK ✓
5. ION ✗
6. DRUMS
7. LIPS
8. READ

53. A query-um...

Move two 'fish' to their correct positions to leave two 7s showing.

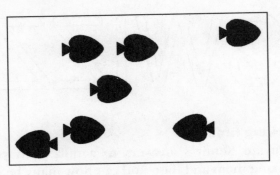

54. Unidentified flying object

Ufologist Wolf Starman recently took this snapshot of the night sky over the infamous UFO hotspot *Area 51*. As well as the Moon and 10 stars it also shows a UFO, but, unfortunately, it looks exactly like a star. Despite this, see if you can still identify it.

55. ✓ Off-the-wall

This wall clock has just fallen on the floor. As a result, its face is badly cracked and the piece to which the hands are attached is missing. Despite this, can you figure out where on earth the clock's hands are (9 letters)?

56. ✓ Letter series

Rearrange one letter below to leave a simple series.

J V W X U Z

57. Take note

On Christmas morning Santa leaves you this note:

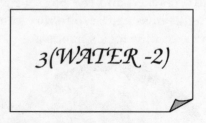

What does it mean?

58. Tricky Ricky

Ricky loses a leg and becomes choosy. Do you know why?

59. Going bananas!

Strawberry Potts, the greengrocer, sells her bananas at the very reasonable price of £1 per pound. So why does the slogan outside her shop say the following?

*MY BANANAS ARE £4 LB. THE BEST
ONES AROUND!*

60. Hybrid

What living animal is a cross between a man and a cat (4 and 3 letters)?

61. Ship out

What type of ship is missing from this list of letters?

BRMUDATAGE

62. Getting on

A friend and I board a bus to go into town. If I am the first person to get on the bus and she is the third person to get on, who is the second person to get on?

63. Four-letter word

Which is the missing word?

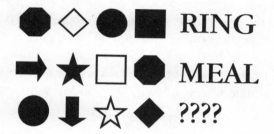

Choose from:

A T O M, C A S E, D I C E, F I S H, G O A L

64. The eight of diamonds

Can you find another eight hidden amongst these diamonds?

65.   CLONED

If the number of cloned sheep on a farm is between 150 and 500, how many are there?

66.   Wonderland wind-up

Alice and the White Rabbit were sitting at an empty tea table. 'If you please, sir,' said Alice nervously. 'If tea is, as you say, at three o'clock on your watch, would you please tell me where it is? It is now after half past three and I'm getting rather hungry!'

'Why,' replied the White Rabbit, getting slightly wound up, 'it's still at three o'clock, of course!'

Poor Alice was confused. Do you know where it is?

67. Missing word
Which is the missing word?

TRANCE is to RADIO

WINCH is to ?

Choose from:

BALLOON, GUILE, JAPAN, MELLOW, RIFLE

68. Easy when you know how
Can you fill in the two missing letters?

69. Seeing double
Below are two identical houses. Take away one match and move another to leave a pair of something else.

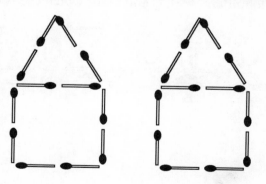

70. An occupational hazard

I was sitting in the bar of the Lateral Thinker's Head recently when in walked a stranger and ordered a drink. The barman handed it to him and said, 'I bet I can guess what job you do.'

'OK', said the man dubiously. 'You write down what you think I do on that piece of paper and I'll write down what I actually do on this piece. We'll then compare notes. If you're correct, I'll buy you a drink, but if you're wrong, you buy me one. Agreed?'

'You're on!' said the barman, reaching for a pen.

When both men had finished writing, the barman looked over at what the man had put. 'See', he said, 'you are a T E.'

Surprisingly, the barman then bought the man a drink. I never did find out the man's occupation. Do you know what it is?

71. Tomb raider

Deep inside the ancient tomb of Queen Gemini a thief is searching for some booty, namely a priceless jewel at the centre of a decorative eye on one of four beautiful candleholders, A, B, C and D. In which eye is the booty?

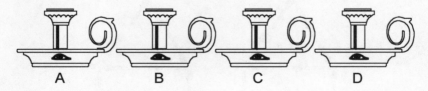

72. What you see is what you get

From what gemstones have the three jewels on this ring been created?

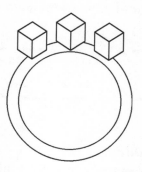

73. Bar trick

Ned goes into his local pub and arranges three plastic counters on the bar as shown below. He then challenges Bill the barman to move one of them so that each is left touching exactly two other counters. After a little while Bill reluctantly gives up and Ned explains how it can be done. How is it possible?

74. Monster puzzle

A man goes into a store and is turned into a space monster. Explain.

75. On the box

Caroline recently bought a secondhand tea chest in perfect condition in an antique shop. Can you rearrange thirteen matches below to recreate her 'mint' tea chest?

— — —   — — — —

— — —   — — — — —

76. Round the table

Can you work out who is round this table?

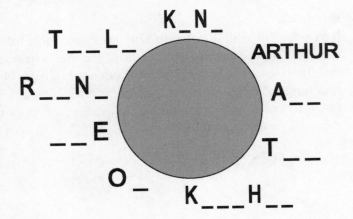

77. **Twin peeks**

Jasmine's two best pals, Josh and Phoenix, are twins and always look identical. They even wear identical looking clothes. While walking to school recently she noticed one of them walking along in the same direction just ahead of her. Not knowing whether it was Josh or Phoenix, she called out 'Hi there!' and, as soon as he turned to face her, she knew that it was Phoenix. How did she know?

78. **Catch me if you can**

Rearrange the letters in one of the groups of letters below to leave a type of fish.

WTHY   NTFH   R

HWL   HFT   KNMSPCF

CBMA   SDYH   MVFD

79. **Final result**

Can you complete the following word just by adding E once?

S QU NCE

80. **Anna-gram**

Anna's favourite dessert contains two ingredients. Unscramble the letters below to find out what they are (6, 3 and 10 letters).

ANNA DOWNS TONS CLOVES

81. Nothing to it

Without changing this equation in any way, can you make it correct?

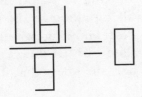

82. Key word

Rearrange three of the matches in this key to leave something unusually hard to enter.

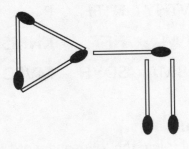

83. Puzzle

What is the missing letter?

84. Get cracking

Max was trying to decipher a 12-letter word in which the letters had been substituted for shapes, but he unfortunately had no decoder. Can you figure out what the word is?

85. Odd man out

Which of these four figures is the odd man out?

86. **A hard nut to crack**

Can you correctly arrange the two missing squares in the last box?

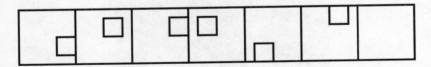

87. **Catwalk**

Below is a cat facing to the left. Move one match to leave a cat the same way up, but going from left to right.

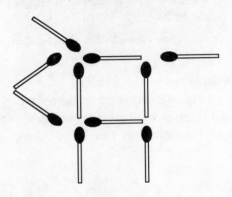

88. **What am I?**

If m_____ is a type of metal and ____j____ is a god, what is _v_____: a tree, a country, a fruit, a goddess or a colour?

89. No butts

Smokey and Puffin can make a whole cigarette from every six cigarette ends that they find. So far today they have managed to collect 92 and 99 ends, and from these they can make none. How come?

90. Capital

Rearrange these four shapes to leave a vertically symmetric capital E with three prongs of equal length. None of the shapes may overlap.

91. ✓ All in order

Place these letters in order and leave a familiar phrase.

UTOFO

92. Marathon man

In 490 BC Pheidippides ran the 20 miles from Marathon to Athens to bring news of the Greek victory over the Persians in the Battle of Marathon. After running the first 17 miles at a constant speed of 10 mph, he inevitably lost some **mph over the last three miles, yet still managed to finish the journey in exactly two hours. How was this possible?

93. ✓ Wild card

Each of these 12 playing cards is covering a different letter of the alphabet in a familiar phrase. Can you figure out what the phrase is and where the missing card is? Watch out, though, as the answer jumps out at you!

94. UFO

Where exactly is the UFO heading?

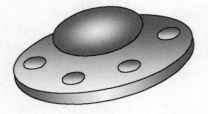

95. Labouring under a misapprehension

Every time Hans walks past the town hall clock in his Austrian home town, he sees the same three labourers sweeping around it, no matter how bad the weather or the lateness of the hour. It's not their job or a punishment, and they're not doing it for charity, so why do they do it?

96. Excellent!

Which two letters should replace the question marks?

WENLELDO??

97. The Time Machine

H G Wells was penning his latest book *The Time Machine*. On his writing desk stood a letter and glass next to each other. What sort of clock was on the desk?

98. On the move

First move a line to create the letter T and then remove that line to leave the letter F.

99. Lift

A woman returning home after a hard day at the office gets a lift from the basement car park of a high-rise building to her apartment, which is on the ground floor. Between the basement and her apartment the lift breaks down, and although it takes half an hour to get it working again, she arrives at her apartment just five minutes later than she would have done had it not broken down. What is the explanation?

100. A mist-erious message

One foggy morning in Oxford Dr Watson receives this message from Sherlock Holmes:

WATSON, MEET ME IN LONDON AT BAKER STATION FRIDAY AFTERNOON – HOLMES

He is very confused by the message because there is no place called Baker Station in London and it doesn't appear to give a time. Where should Dr Watson meet Holmes and at what time?

Answers to easy puzzles

Scoring and creativity rating

Award yourself one point for each of the puzzles in the easy section that you get correct, and two points for each of the puzzles in the hard section that you get correct, including two points for each of the six rebuses in question 66. The total number of possible points is 310.

250+	Super creative genius
200–249	Creative genius
150–199	Potential creative genius
100–149	Extremely creative
50–99	Very creative
20–49	Above average
1–19	Average

Answers

1. 'Minute' was pronounced 'my newt' by grandma.
2. A cove. A(**d**)mire, A(**d**)minister, A(**l**)cove, A(**d**)vent, A(**d**)verse.
3. Fill in the rest of the letter As to leave BANANA.

4. EL-EM-EN-TARY.
5. The CAB below the three taxis is out of order.
6. None because the symbol on the card is the wrong way up to be a heart. It is, in fact, an unfinished spade.
7. Just leave a dot because 'a dot' is a sort of 'toad'.
8. Arrange the three words to get FARMER SUE TICKLES, which sounds like 'pharmaceuticals'.
9. Croft. C(3) + R(18) + O(15) + ft.
10. ANGLE. TO OPEN THE DOOR TRY-ANGLE (TRIANGLE).
11. R and E. MAN + EYE(I) + KIN = MANIKIN, RAN + SEA(C) + OUR = RANCOUR and FIG + EWE(U) + RED = FIGURED.

12.   Move the bottom match to leave a square zero.

13.   m.

> **One** potato, **two** potato, **three** potato, **four,**
> **Five** potato, **six** potato, **seven** potato **more.**

14.   2 mushrooms.

15.   Rearrange one match as shown below to leave VI (6)
      AITCHES. The seventh H is contained in the word
      AITCH itself.

16. V to leave SNOWMAN upside-down.

17. MOON. The others contain Bs or Bees.

18. Add the letters in DASHES to leave DAISYWHEELS going clockwise.

19. Fountain pen (anagram of Anton Fepuni).

20. PEARLS can be found directly above the letters of ISLAND on the map.

21. Fingers, thumbs and toes.

22. The unoccupied squares form the word count.

23. THESE and ARE. The word is PARENTHESES.

24. HALIBUT.

25. Times Square:

26. She leaves with 20 minus 1 (twenty–one) pound coins or 19 pounds, which is the correct amount.

27. Treat the times as ratios so that 5:10 becomes 5 to 10 and 10:12 becomes 10 to 12.

28. He. All of the others are the first two letters of a month.

29. A vegetable. d = Dee, b = bee and p = pea.

30.

31.   Lake Huron.

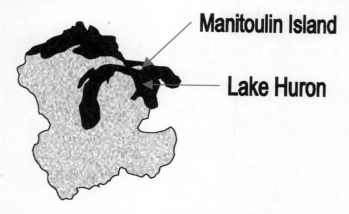

32.   Sam as in Uncle Sam. **UNITED STATES OF AMERICA**.
33.   You stick a match in an orange to make a match stick out of it.
34.   R and R. ABRACADABRA can be found going in an anti-clockwise direction.
35.   Notwithstanding.

36. Just turn the match around like this so that the match is left facing in the opposite direction.

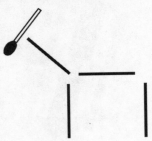

37. MIL+LI ON.
38. It actually takes off at one (half two).
39. Ohio. O high o.
40. It has a tick formed by its hands.
41.

42. Seven are achieved by simply rearranging the top cube in seven different ways to spell OWL. The eighth, however, is achieved like this:

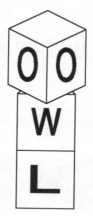

43. SPACE.
44. A Toyota. A to Y ot (back to) A.
45. Each matchstick has two sides showing so there are actually just four matches in all, with three in group A and one in group B. It is therefore just a simple matter of moving one match from group A to group B.
46. KEY because it may be appended to DON to give DON-KEY and because it may be used to start a car.
47. Potatoes (pot eight Os).
48. Rotate the 2 discs with Es on them to create the word DECODED on its side.

49.   Ironside (i on side).

50.   A. Ignore the changing dots and you'll see that the boxes contain the word NEWNESS.

51.

52.   Kenny got five correct.

1. COARSE✓ (CAUSTIC)
2. ACROSS✓ (ACROSTIC)
3. VICTORIA✗ (VICTORIA CROSS)
4. ARK✓ (ARCTIC)
5. ION✗ (IRON CROSS)
6. DRUMS✓ (DRUMSTICK)
7. LIPS✓ (LIPSTICK)
8. READ✗ (RED CROSS)

53.

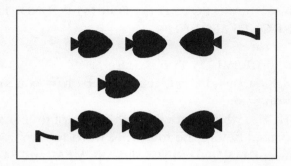

54. If the circled spot were a star, it would be obscured by the dark side of the moon. Therefore, this spot must be the UFO.

55. Antarctic. The cracked clock face is a view of the Earth.

56.

57. HO HO HO (3 X H2O – 2).

58. If you remove a 'leg' from the R of Ricky, you get Picky.

59. Interpreted correctly the slogan actually says: MY BANANAS ARE POUND (£) FOR (4) POUND (LB.) THE BEST ONES AROUND!

60. Manx cat.

61. LINER. BERMUDA TRIANGLE.

62. You. First person = I, second person = you and third person = she.

63. FISH. The white shape in each group of four shapes can be placed before the following word to form a word or phrase: DIAMOND RING, SQUARE MEAL and STARFISH.

64. The other eight can be seen between the diamonds on the eight of diamonds.

65. One. CL-ONE-D.

66. The tea he referred to is the letter T on its side on the right side of his watch at 3 o'clock.

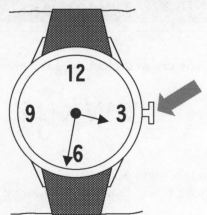

67. RIFLE. When read out loud the top line sounds like TRANSISTOR RADIO and the bottom one like WINCH-ESTER RIFLE.

68. Remove the numbers in the circles to leave these three words:

O M I N O U S
O U T D O N E
O B V I O U S

69.

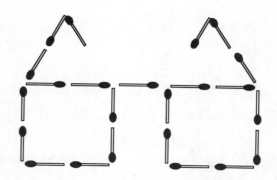

70. Curate. The barman spelt out C-U-R-A-T-E.

71. The booty is in the eye of the B holder (The beauty is in the eye of the beholder).

72. Diamonds because each cube is created from three diamond shapes.

73. Place the left counter on the other two so that it is then touching two other counters. Each of the other two counters is then touching two other counters as well if you include the bar or counter beneath them.

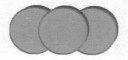

74. Place the letters of MAN into STORE and then rearrange them to form A MONSTER which is A SPACE MONSTER.

75. Rearrange the letters in THIRTEEN MATCHES to get:

<u>H</u> E <u>R</u> <u>M</u> <u>I</u> <u>N</u> <u>T</u>

<u>T</u> E <u>A</u> <u>C</u> H E <u>S</u> <u>T</u>

76. KING ARTHUR AND THE KNIGHTS OF THE ROUND TABLE.

77. Josh is deaf.

78.

WTHY   NTFH   R
N   S   C
HWL   HFT   K
M   P   F
CBMA   SDYH   MVFD

79. Add the letters in E ONCE to get CONSEQUENCE.

80. VOWELS AND CONSONANTS.

81. Obl-on-g = □.

82. Rearrange the matches to form a tetrahedron, which is an anagram of HARD TO ENTER.

83. B. Superimpose the nine boxes to get RUBIK CUBE reading across from left to right.

84. DODECAHEDRON, which is an anagram of HAD NO DECODER.

85. TOMMY. The others are formed from the letters of women's names: POLLY, SONYA and MOLLY.

86. The boxes contain the word coconut.

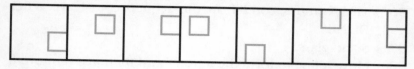

87.

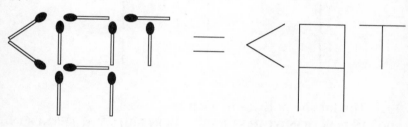

88. A goddess. m_____ = Mercury, ____j____ = Jupiter, _v_____ = Venus

89. NINETY-TWO + NINETY-NINE ends = NONE.

90.

91. O(UT OF O)RDER.
92. He lost some oomph, but not speed.
93. JACK-IN-THE-BOX.
94. The UFO heading is the puzzle's title.
95. They are the town hall clock's hands.
96. The N and second E in the sequence to leave WELL DONE.
97. S-and-glass.
98. Move a line to form the letter T and then just re-move it (ie move it again) to form the letter F.

99. The lift she got was in a car.
100. IN LONDON AT BAKER ST-AT-I-ON FRIDAY AFTERNOON.

Creative thinking test 1

The following 20 questions have been designed to test your creative thinking ability. Allow yourself an hour of uninterrupted time to attempt them.

1. Can you put the spot in the correct position in this number?

2. Can you find the saying below?

    G is a NY

3. What is the next number in this sequence?

    12, 37, 51, 93, 41, 23, 75, 19, 34, ??

4. Connect a total of seven spots with eight more straight lines to make a familiar object.

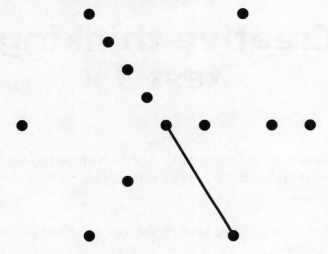

5. What familiar phrase is represented below?

    ## A. Why said on Jung, 'Shoal does.'

6. Take away one line to leave a fish going north-east.

7. What is the next letter in this sequence?

    ## REQLPFO?

8. Fill in the four missing circles in the last grid.

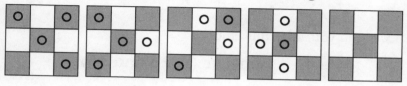

9. Move the two black T-shapes to leave the word HI. You may not rotate the shapes.

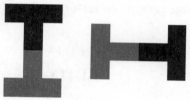

10. What familiar phrase does this rebus represent (4 and 7 letters)?

    BATT_R

11. Choose a number (1–10) to continue this series.

    6, 3, 0, –3, –6, ?

12. Move two lines to leave '80'.

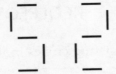

13. Can you solve this clue?

A film star (2, 18 and 15)

14. If E + M = O°, what are E and M?

15. Insert a different letter from the word LAMP in each of the following groups of letters to leave a familiar series of words.

ALOHA

BETO

GAMOA

DEOTA

16.

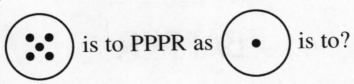

Choose from:

ADB, FKR, JYR, PWR, SLT

17. Which one of the following is a bird of prey?

> A stork
> B dove
> C raven
> D puffin
> E gull
> F robin

18. Find the odd one out.

B z 8 E U o

19. Try to fill in the missing letters to complete this phrase. Hint: It has an 'H' at each end.

> _ _ G _ _ / _ _ E _ _

20. What should replace the question mark?

⌐⌐ ⌐⌐ ?⌐ ⌐⌐ ⌐⌐

Answers to creative thinking test 1

1.

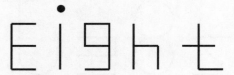

2. Rearrange the letters in 'G is a NY' to get SAYING.
3. 12. The same sequence of nine digits is repeated.
4.

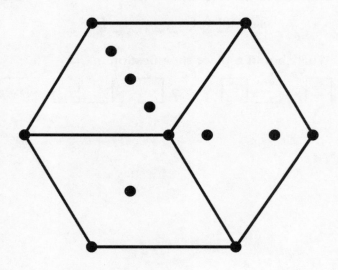

5. Read it out loud to get 'a wise head on young shoulders'.

6. Take away a line to leave the word EEL like this:

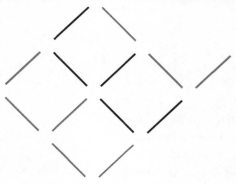

7. I. Each letter appears four positions further on minus a line.

8. In each successive grid the shaded squares contain one less circle and the white squares contain one more circle.

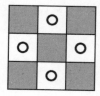

9.

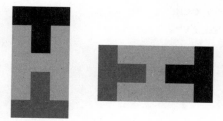

10. Flat battery.

11. −9. 1 − 10 = −9.

12. '80' sounds like 'a T'.

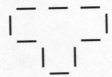

13. Brando. B (2), R (18) and O (15).

14. E = Earth and M = Moon.

15. Put the letters in the circles to get AL(P)HA, BET(A), GAM(M)A and DE(L)TA.

16. SLT. The diagrams are the tops of pepper and salt pots. PPPR and SLT are PEPPER and SALT without the vowels.

17. E gull because it sounds like eagle.

18. The six figures are created from the letters in ODD ONE OUT.

19. RUGBY FIELD.

20. Move each pair of 'letters' together to form the sequence 6, 5, 4, 3, 2 on its side.

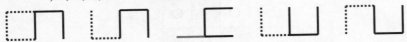

Creativity rating

1–5   Average
6–10   Above average
11–15 Very creative
16–20 Extremely creative

PART 2

Hard puzzles

Introduction to hard puzzles

The puzzles in this section are a little more difficult than the ones in the previous section, and to solve them, you will need to call upon every one of your newly acquired creative thinking skills. However, if you remember to keep an open mind and allow your intuition to guide you, you will probably be surprised at just how well you do. To give you an idea of what to expect, here are a couple of examples:

Example 1.   Series
What number should replace the question mark below?

O3 •7 •5 •5 •4 •7 •6 •6 •7 •?

Example 2.   Building block
Move two of these five toothpicks to leave a view of a famous US building.

Answers

Example 1.   5. The circle and spots represent the sun and the nine planets in the solar system, and the numbers represent the number of letters in each of their names.

Example 2.   Arrange the two toothpicks to create an overhead view of the Pentagon like this:

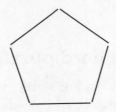

Now try the rest of the puzzles.

1. Monolith

This mysterious monolith was recently discovered on the planet Mars. How tall is it?

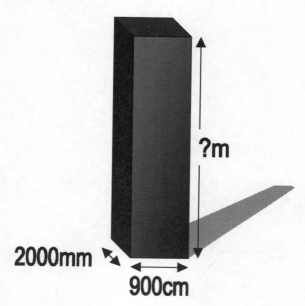

2000mm ✕ ◀▶ **900cm**

?m

2. What lies beneath

Replace the question marks with numbers to leave this equation correct. Assume that the first digit of each missing number is not 0.

$$\frac{8}{????} + \frac{5}{?????} + \frac{2}{??} + \frac{1}{???} + \frac{7}{?????} = \frac{7}{32}$$

3. **Bravo!**
   What two-letter word should replace the question marks?

NO

GARLIC

RUN!

ANGELS

TURIN

UNTO

LITERATI

??

4. **Watch out!**
   An explorer notices a poisonous snake at 3 o'clock on his watch. What type of snake is it?

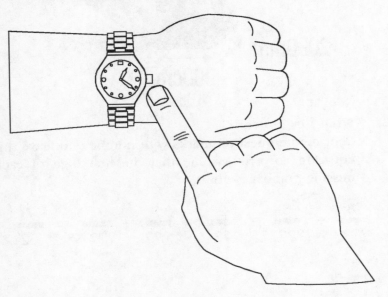

5. Letter sequence

Which other circle should be black to complete the sequence below?

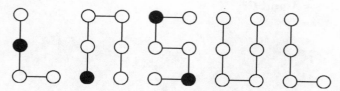

6. Time travel

Early one morning Dan checks that his watch is correct and then leaves his home to visit his friend Ben. On reaching Ben's house, Ben points out that Dan's watch is one hour slow and so Dan puts it right. When Dan arrives back at his home later on in the day he sees that his watch is again showing the wrong time. But without any assistance whatsoever, he puts his watch exactly right. How is this possible?

7. **A different slant**

    A, B, C and D are four sleeping ladybugs on a perfectly flat tabletop. What is the direct distance between ladybugs A and C?

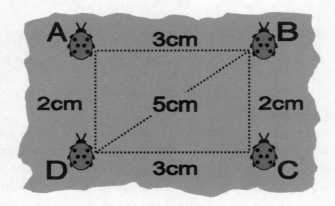

8. **Bermuda short**

On the afternoon of 11 December you awake in your cabin aboard your luxury yacht in the notorious Bermuda Triangle. Being unable to hear the crew, you decide to venture out and look for them. But you cannot find them, so, feeling slightly puzzled, you return to your cabin. It is then that you look up at this clock, which immediately suggests to you a well-known expression possibly explaining their whereabouts. What is this expression (3, 5, 2 and 4 letters)?

9. **The big breakfast**

A waitress in a diner goes up to a man eating his breakfast.

Waitress: Reg?

Man: No. I'll have two more eggs please.

What exactly did the waitress ask the man (3, 4, 4 and 5 letters)?

10. Take it away!

Take away one line from this arrangement to leave 3!

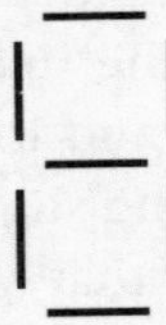

11. Trendsetter

What six-letter word is missing from this sequence?

DIRECT

ROLE

OCCIDENTAL

DARE

??????

SHADOW

AMUSED

12. Cube

Move one match to leave a cube with each of the six numbers one to six represented once.

13. Home alone

Which home below is incomplete?

A   B   C   D   E

14. Houston, we have a problem

Can you help Luke Spacewalker place the remaining four letters correctly in the grid?

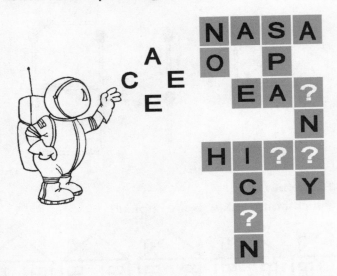

15. After eights

What comes next in this series of eights?

Choose from:

     A   B   C   D   E

16. **An arranged marriage**

Prince Olav wishes to marry the beautiful Princess Tatyana and so her father, King Hargnor, sets him a challenge to prove his worthiness as a suitor. He instructs Olav to turn over one of the three cards on the right, only one of which he is told has a letter on its reverse side, and place it beneath the three cards on the left to form a new English word reading down. Hargnor, however, doesn't really want Tatyana to marry Olav and so the reverse sides of all three cards are left blank. Olav, however, forewarned of this by Tatyana, still somehow manages to make a new word by turning over one of the cards on the right and placing it below the other three on the left. Which card — A, B or C – does he turn over and what word does he create?

17. Subtraction

Take away four matchsticks to leave just two.

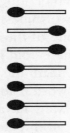

18. Four-gone conclusion

Take away four of these small triangles and yet somehow still leave a capital E.

19. Bob along

Rearrange one line inside each end box to leave BOB.

20. Off with their heads!

Below is a headless match. Add another headless match to leave the letter H. You may not bend or break any matches.

21. Final destination

I start at the fifth floor, then go to the third floor, then the fourth floor and then, finally, the first floor to get exactly where in a building (4 letters)?

22. Alphabet tickle

Take away one of the letters in this grid and yet still leave all 26 letters of the alphabet.

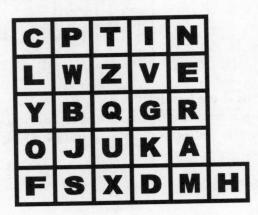

23. Spot check

Logically, what should replace the question marks?

$$1:3::5:?7?$$

24. Getting away with murder

A security guard in a hotel sees a man go alone into a room in which there is no one else present and which may only be accessed through a single doorway. Several minutes later he sees a second person, a woman, enter the room and then scream. Lying dead on the floor of the room in a pool of blood is the man and it is obvious he has been murdered. But how does the killer manage to get in and out of the room without being seen by the guard, who remains on the same spot and watchful throughout?

25. Pony

A pony is staring at its reflection in a stream. Suddenly a gust of wind blows away eight of the matches leaving just a pony. How is this possible?

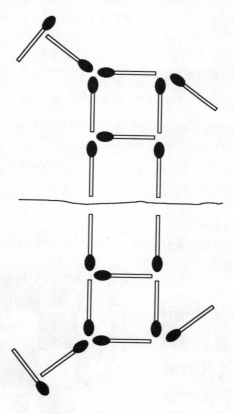

26. Whodunnit
Pandora, Harry, Alec, Gemima and Geoffrey are animals in a zoo. The other day one of them ate an animal called Tabitha. Who ate her and what type of animal was it?

? ATE HER

27. Give me five!

5, 10, 15, 20, 25, 30, 35, ?

Can you find the number below that comes next in the above series?

6, 15, 18, 20, 25

28. Where's queen?
On which black square is the black queen?

Q = BLACK QUEEN
K = WHITE KING
R = BLACK ROOK
P = WHITE PAWN
B = BLACK BISHOP

29. **A twist in the tail**

Move one match to leave Charlie the reindeer looking to his right.

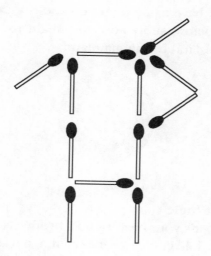

30. **Car**

Can you fill in the rest of the letters to complete this car?

_ _ A R _ I _ / _ L _ _ A / R O M E O

31. **Catnap**

The sheep at Sleepy Farm sleep under a tree, the cattle sleep in the barn, the horses sleep in the stables and the dog sleeps in the farmhouse. By the sound of things, the cat will sleep where?

32. Stick around

You are stranded on a small circular island in the middle of a large, deep piranha-infested lake. The only thing you have to help you escape is a cane. Using the diagram below, show how you might use a cane to get from the island to the mainland.

33. A leap of logic

'So, Sally, it's your best friend's brother's birthday today and you'd like me to make him a cake', says Aunt Dorothy. 'Do you know how old he is today, as I really need to know how many candles to put on it?'

'Not exactly', replies Sally. 'But I do know that he's between nine and fifteen years old inclusive.'

'Thanks', says Aunt Dorothy. 'Now I know how old he is.'

Assuming Aunt Dorothy puts one candle on the cake for every year of his age, how many does she need?

34. It's a steal

Hannah's red smock has been stolen by one of her six pets, Bat, Cat, Hen, Owl, Ram and Rat. To help you solve the case you need Doctor Watson and Sherlock Holmes.

??? stole Hannah's red smock

Which pet stole Hannah's smock?

35. Cryptic crossword

What are the two missing letters?

ACROSS
3) 6 across and 4 down
6) 9 across and 4 down
8) 2 across and 4 down

DOWN
1) 2 down and 4 across
2) 3 down and 5 across
4) 2 down and 2 across
5) 4 down and 7 across
7) 3 down and 7 across

36. Points in time

'Jessica, what time are the hour and minute hands of the clock pointing to?' asks Joe. She looks at the clock and then writes down the following:

1:21 exactly and 1:25 approximately.

What time does the clock say?

37. Don't jump to the wrong conclusion!

A cat burglar is on the roof of apartment block A and needs to get onto the roof of apartment block B to evade an elderly security guard, who is chasing him. Between the two roofs is a five metre long plank, which only just reaches the edge of each building. Unfortunately, though, it is unsafe so he cannot use it to cross over. So if he can only long jump four metres, how come he is easily able to get across and evade the guard?

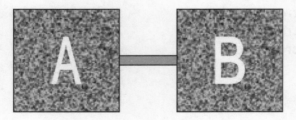

38. Sign of the times

After this clock says five it says five before one, then five before two, then three after five and then ten after one. Can you guess what it says next?

39. Holiday destination

Arrange the letters TRS and EDA either side of these letters to find out my favourite holiday destination.

HEE

40. Message in a bottle

What does the message in this bottle say?

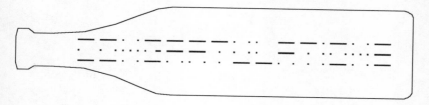

41. Dial-bolical

First find the hidden logic and then figure out which dial is incorrect.

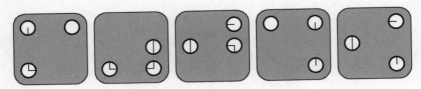

42. Silence her!

An off-duty police officer is walking past a motel room when he hears a man's voice in the room call out: 'Quickly, silence her!' Without hesitating the officer pulls out his gun and bursts into the room, where he finds two unfamiliar men, each clutching a revolver, standing at one end and a woman lying dead on the floor with a bullet hole in her head at the other. Surprised by his sudden entrance both men instinctively put up their hands, and while neither of their guns is still giving off any telltale smoke, the officer immediately knows who shot the victim. How come?

43. Cube

Rearrange three of these four digital segments to turn this square number into a cube, but not 1. None of the segments may overlap.

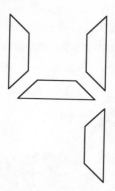

44. Roller coaster

What is the next letter in this series?

45. Time bomb

Originally this clock had three complete hands, but as you can see, part of the second hand has broken off. Apart from this it is in perfect working order and correct. Given that the dynamite is set to explode at precisely three o'clock and that it takes twenty-one seconds to defuse, how come you are easily able to make it safe in time?

46. Ladybugs

Six ladybugs are lying fast asleep side by side between two flowers. What is the distance between the two flowers?

47. Christmas time

It is late on Christmas Eve and little Holly is waiting for the Christmas tree to be finished. At exactly what time will this happen?

48. Anagram

Solve this anagram. (5, 8, 5 and 12 letters):

NOTIONAL ATTAINING TRAY ORCHESTRA

49. Magic power

Batwinkle the wizard adds 27 identical cubes together to form a large cube. Then, without touching the sides of the large cube, he takes away the centre cube to leave 26. How does he do it?

50. On the cards

You shouldn't have much trouble finding the six of spades below, but can you find the six of hearts, diamonds and clubs?

51. Gap year

Add 500 to the top row and 100 to the bottom row so that the latter predates the former.

A 1502

B 1902

52. Die-hard

Rearrange these six equilateral triangles to create a view of a regular die.

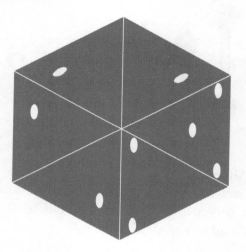

53. Schoolwork

Add the eight shapes that make up the two fish on the right to the arrangement of seven fish on the left to leave an equal number of fish of the same shape facing in opposite directions. None of the shapes may overlap, no fish shapes may be formed by spaces between the shapes and no shapes should be redundant.

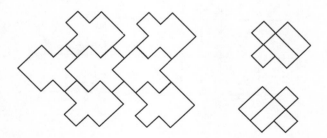

54. Sixth sense

What comes next in this match sequence?

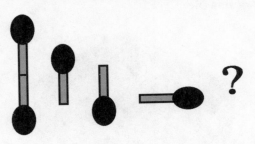

55. Long division

What well-known geographical feature, found on maps of the United States, is represented by the letters and symbols in this grid?

V	L	+	T	+	L	T
+	T	L	V	+	T	+
L	L	+	V	T	+	L
+	L	L	V	+	T	L
+	T	L	+	V	T	+
V	V	T	+	L	L	V
+	V	T	V	+	L	=

56. A spot of bother

Add six black spots to complete this view of a die.

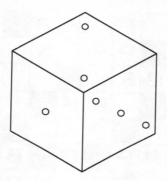

57. Snowman

Which month is indicated in this wintery scene: April, May, June, July or August?

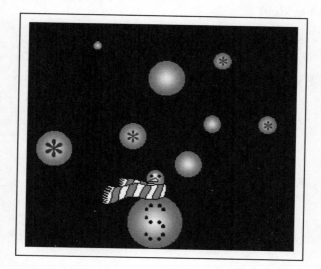

58. Check it out!

Fill in the appropriate squares to complete this grid.

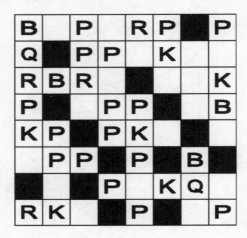

59. A big deal

Fill in the missing letters in this sequence.

??E, TWO, THREE, FOUR, FIVE, SIX,
SEVEN, EIGHT, NINE, TEN, ????, ???EN, ?IN?

60. Safe play

Turn the dial on this safe 180 degrees clockwise, then 90 degrees counterclockwise, and then 45 degrees clockwise, to reveal a single item of jewellery (7 and 4 letters).

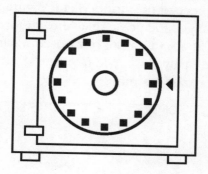

61. A wolf in sheep's clothing
Which word goes at the end?

bales canal baled bated level ?

Choose from:

paled, baked, sheep, banal, chain

62. Last minute change

One night a man is shot dead with a single bullet which shatters the clock on the wall behind him. The next morning a detective arrives on the scene. When he first sees this piece of the stopped clock lying on the floor he immediately concludes that the shooting must have occurred at about 11.06, but on closer inspection, that it must actually have taken place at about 2.20. Why does he change his mind?

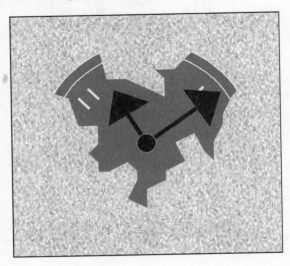

63. Watch it!

If watches A and B equal 2 and 3 o'clock respectively, what time does watch C equal: 4, 5, 6, 7 or 8 o'clock?

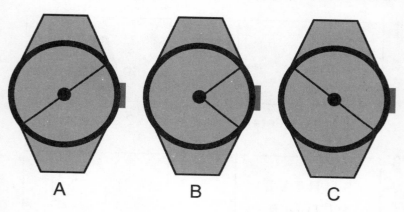

A   B   C

64. The great divide

Rearrange the four digits on the left side of this sum so that the answer is still four.

$$68 \div 17 = 4$$

65. Re-phrase

All except for one of the first four words are repeated in the following well-known phrase. What is the phrase?

??? ??? ??? ??? ??? ??? ???

66. Rebuses

What well-known phrase or saying is represented by each of these rebuses?

1

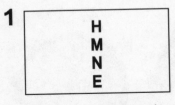

(1,7 and 5 letters)

2

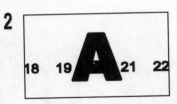

(1,6,2 and 7 letters)

3

(2,2,4,3,3 and 5 letters)

4

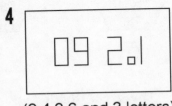

(2,4,2,6 and 3 letters)

5

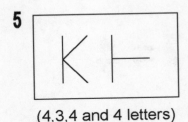

(4,3,4 and 4 letters)

6

D_ ARTH

(5 and 7 letters)

67. Fighting fit
Can you fill in the missing word?

1 ECO
2 IRE
3 IGLOO
4 SEAL
5 ????
6 FUN

68. Solar system
Can you fill in the missing letters in this solar system?

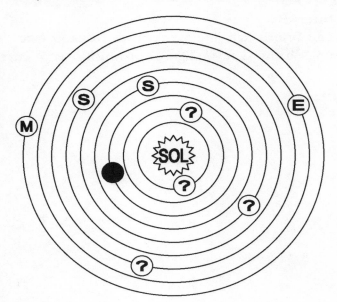

69. **Insider dealing**
    What is the missing word?

    R6P9 = BIRD

    bPR = UNUSUAL

    Rd = ?

    Choose from:

    ACT, BEETLE, GHOST, JUMP, POLAR

70. **Inter-city**
    The British Rail line Startstop to Laststop takes in an English city. Can you figure out which one (7 letters)?

71. As if by magic

On one side of the table a poor magician arranges the last five of his copper coins. Next, he puts the first four coins on the other side of the table and, as if by magic, one other copper coin appears. Using the diagram below, can you show how this trick might be achieved?

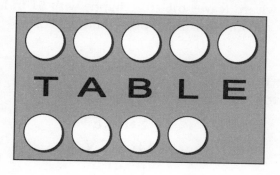

72. Part exchange

You have 6 x 4 x 25 identical small wooden cubes. How can you add two single cubes to this large number of small wooden cubes to enable you to create one large wooden cube using all of them?

73. Sidewalk

What letter should replace the question mark?

74. **Down payment**

A wizard pops into his local magic store to buy a new pet toad. Unfortunately, he only has £2 on him and the toad costs quite a bit more than this, so he asks the shopkeeper if he can pay £1 now and the rest the following week. The kind shopkeeper agrees to this and the wizard leaves the store happy with £1 in his pocket and a toad. How much does the toad cost?

75. **The last word**

What is the missing three-letter word?

SHINE

LICHEN

POSER

DICE

EXODUS

NARWHAL

RAMP

???

76. **Reported speech**

This is Emily's account of a puzzling conversation she recently overheard between two of her college pals:

Mandy: 'Lucy, how old is your sister, Sarah?'

Lucy: 'She's between 13 and 20 inclusive.'

Mandy: 'Could you be a little more specific?'

Lucy: 'If I tell you that she's not 18, you'll know just how old she is.'

Can you figure out Sarah's age?

77. Figure it out

Which figure comes next in this sequence?

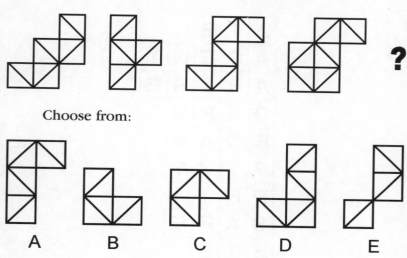

Choose from:

A   B   C   D   E

78. Death of a reporter

A reporter is found lying outside the new Tate art centre. What is the cause of death (5 and 6 letters)?

79. **Word search**

What is the missing word?

80. **Far out!**

Can you make this equation correct without changing it in any way?

$$1\% + 200 = 3\%$$

81. **Trouble in store**

A man goes into a grocery store in downtown San Francisco and asks the shopkeeper if he has any **n*e**u*. The shopkeeper replies rather rudely: 'I don't have any, man. Get out!' What did the man ask for?

82. Letter boxes

Add the three boxes on the right to the arrangement of boxes on the left to make the letter H.

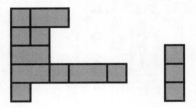

83. Diameters

Are the lines AB and CD 6meters, 72meters, 102meters, 491meters, 734meters or 813meters?

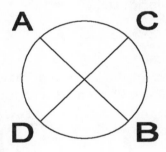

84. Betweentimes

Gerald arrives at his local railway station to catch the Waterloo train, which departs hourly at exactly five minutes past the hour. Thinking he might have just missed it, he looks up at the station clock and sees that the hour and minute hands are coincident between 1 and 2. Surprisingly, he then knows that he hasn't missed his train. If the clock is correct, how does he know?

85. Play your card right

Move only one of these cards to leave a fourth jack.

86. Coincidence

Having first put down some money, I then toss the dice. Next I add the number to the score and find that the sum total, coincidentally, is what?

87. Metamorphosis

Rearrange five of the following 'matches' to leave the name of some familiar aquatic creatures.

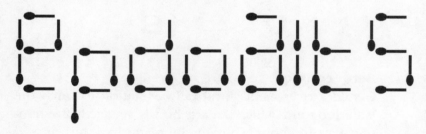

88. **Start over**

Which three consecutive letters of the alphabet can be placed in front of these letters, in alphabetical order, to form an English word?

_ _ _ g h n u t

89. **Jockeying for position**

Three letters, N, E and T, have been removed from this newspaper headline exactly once. Put them back in their original positions, none of which are adjacent, to discover the original headline.

> **SPECTATORS' ROAR**
> **HELPS U.S.A. JOCKEY**
> **IN KENTUCKY DERBY**

90. Hiding-place

Which famous city may be found in the background of this picture?

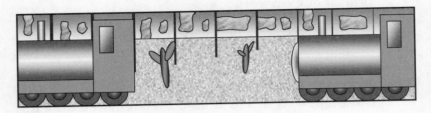

91. Out of the box

Which is the missing square?

92. On your mark

Why is 'P' the only letter of the alphabet missing below?

B C D F G H J L ? V W X Y Z

93. The magic word

After hours of searching the castle you eventually find the mysterious Room 88 at the end of a long gloomy corridor. Appropriately enough, it has 'R88' on it. You try to open the door, but it is locked. Suddenly a ghostly voice from inside murmurs: 'Say the magic word and the door will open.' What word should you say?

94. Grid grind

What should go in the two empty squares?

A₁	I₁	T₁	R₁	H₄	G₂	E₁	N₁	B₃	L₁
I₁	G₂	A₁	C₃	T₁	U₁	O₁	B₃	E₁	I₁
T₁	L₁	E₁	L₁	Q₁₀	D₂	M₃	E₁	S₁	O₁
E₁	N₁	O₁	X₈	R₁	W₄	E₁	A₁	D₂	F₄
P₃	U₁	A₁	I₁	N₁	U₁	O₁	N₁	I₁	O₁
M₃	R₁	O₁	V₄	E₁	Z₁₀	E₁	T₁		P₃
E₁	I₁	S₁	I₁	A₁	D₂	S₁	I₁	A₁	T₁
A₁	R₁	O₁	G₂	N₁	S₁	A₁	E₁	W₄	N₁
E₁	V₄	I₁	D₂	U₁		L₁	E₁	C₃	F₄
H₄	Y₄	K₅	R₁	O₁	J₈	T₁	Y₄	A₁	R₁

95. Eye test

Just add a line to complete the series below.

??? ? ?I? ?? ? ???

96. Age game

Kate: 'How old are you, Carl?'

Carl: 'I'm between 20 and 30 years old.'

Kate: 'Could you be a little more specific?'

Carl writes down two digits, and although neither is the same as either of those in his age, Kate knows exactly how old he is. Do you?

97. A bit of a blast

Fill in the appropriate lines to complete the following.

BOTH

———

———

———

RATION

———

———

———

98. **Crystal clear**

What is the volume of this crystal?

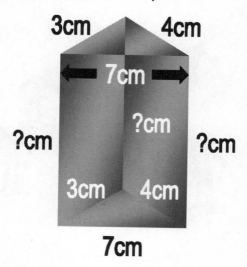

99. **Nothing to choose**

Which same four letters complete these three words?

_ E _ _ R _

_ _ _ U _

_ _ O _ _ U L

Choose from:

ABCDEFGHIJKLMNOPQRSTUVWXYZ

100 A wintery spell

Can you fill in the rest of the letters to complete this
sequence?

Answers to hard puzzles

Scoring and creativity rating

Award yourself one point for each of the puzzles in the easy section that you get correct, and two points for each of the puzzles in the hard section that you get correct, including two points for each of the six rebuses in question 66. The total number of possible points is 310.

250+	Super creative genius
200–249	Creative genius
150–199	Potential creative genius
100–149	Extremely creative
50–99	Very creative
20–49	Above average
1–19	Average

Answers

1. 1,000 m. In Roman numerals cm, mm and m equal 900, 2,000 and 1,000 respectively.

2.

$$\frac{8}{1,000} + \frac{5}{100,000} + \frac{2}{10} + \frac{1}{100} + \frac{7}{10,000} = \frac{7}{32}$$

or

$$\frac{2}{10} + \frac{1}{100} + \frac{8}{1,000} + \frac{7}{10,000} + \frac{5}{100,000} = 0,21875$$

3. AT. Start at C and read in a counterclockwise direction around the outside of the list of words to find CONGRATULATIONS!

NO

GARLIC

RUN!

ANGELS

TURIN

UNTO

LITERATI

AT

4. A sidewinder (side winder).

5.

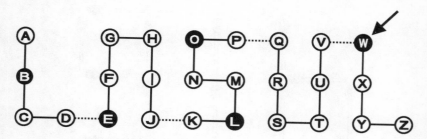

6.   Ben lives in a time zone that is one hour ahead.

7.   1 cm. AB + AD and BC + CD are both equal to BD, so the four ladybugs must actually lie in a straight line as follows:

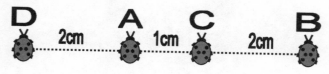

8.   All hands on deck. DEC plus K, the *eleventh* letter of the alphabet.

9.   Are four eggs ample? Are (R) for example (eg).

10.   Factorial 3(3!) is equal to 3 x 2 x 1 or 6.

11.   ANSWER. The middle two letters of each word become the first and last letters of the next one.

12.

13. ABODE. The O in ABCDE is incomplete.

14.

15. D. The sequence is made up of two series of 'E-I-G-H-T-S' spelt out in Morse code with one placed on top of the other.

16. He turns over card A to create the word Logic as follows:

17. Take away the four matchsticks (not matches) to leave a number two as follows:

18. Take away four small triangles to leave either of these three-dimensional views of a capital E.

19.

20.

21. I start at the *fifth* floor, then go to the *third* floor, then the *fourth* floor and then, finally, the *first* floor to get ROOF.

22.

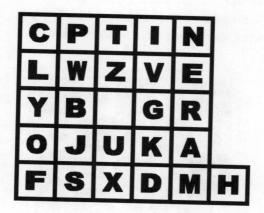

23. :: and :::: to leave the sequence 1:3::5:::7:::: (1, 2, 3, 4, 5, 6, 7, 8).

24. The room is a lift.

25.

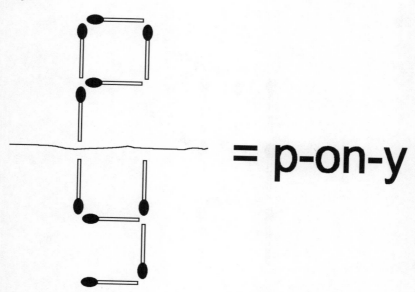

= p-on-y

26. Alec ate her. This sounds like alligator.
27. FORTY. Substitute the numbers 6, 15, 18, 20 and 25 for the corresponding letters in the alphabet.
28.

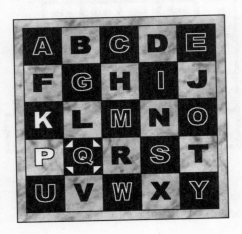

29.

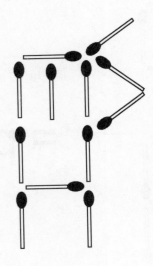

30. **CHARLIE ALPHA** ROMEO. These are the letters of the phonetic alphabet representing C, A and R.

31. In the barn. The phrase 'the cattle sleep in the barn' sounds like 'the cat'll sleep in the barn'.

32.

CANOE

33. 12. It's 29 February so it's a leap year and therefore Aunt Dorothy knows that his age must be divisible by four.

34. Owl. *Doctor* 'Watson and Sherlock Holmes' to get **Owl stole Hannah's red smock.**

35. H and I to make the word HIT. Each clue gives the sum of the number of horizontal (across) and vertical (down) lines comprising its answer's letters.

36. 5:05. Of the two hands, one points (:) to (2) one exactly and one points (:) to (2) five approximately.

37. Apartment block A is at least 3 metres taller than apartment block B and so the horizontal distance the cat burglar has to jump to negotiate the gap between the two buildings is actually only 4 metres or less.

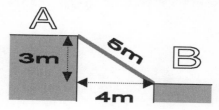

38. Ten. Each of the 'times' is a description of one of the Roman numerals representing the numbers 5 to 10. V = five, VI = five before one, VII = five before two, VIII = three after five, IX = ten after one, X = ten.

39. Arrange them like this to leave THE RED SEA reading down from left to right.

T R S

H E E

E D A

40. It is the tops, middles and bottoms of the letters in CONGRATULATIONS.

41.

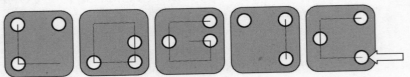

42. One of the men's guns has a silencer (silence her).

43.

44.

45. The actual time is ten seconds after three o'clock. The second hand has a counterbalance.

46. TWO IN-CHES.

47. At midnight when the hands of the clock form a Christmas Tree.

48. NORTH ATLANTIC TREATY ORGANISATION. The initial letters of the words in **NOTIONAL ATTAINING TRAY ORCHESTRA** were a clue.

49. He multiplies the cube number 8 by 27, then removes 1 (1 cubed) from the resultant number 216 to leave 26.

50. The hearts, diamonds and clubs on the 9, 3 and 5 spell 'SIX', giving the 'six of hearts, diamonds and clubs'.

51. Add the Roman numerals D(500) and C(100) to get AD1502 and BC1902.

52. Arrange the triangles like this to create a view showing just 2 sides of a die. 'Die-hard' is based on 'Cubic Hexagon' by Barry R. Clarke.

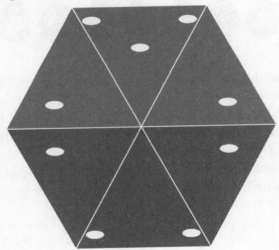

53. Add them like this so that you are left with a total of eight fish of the same shape with four small fish swimming to the right and three small fish and one large fish swimming to the left.

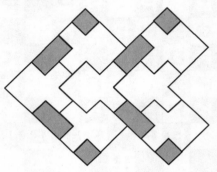

54. The lines form the word HUNCH.

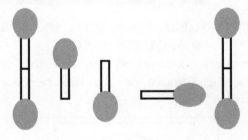

55. The forty-ninth Parallel. The forty-ninth pair of lines in the 49 squares are the only pair of lines that are parallel.
56. Just place the spots in the six circles.
57. JUNE. The snowman and snowballs represent the Sun and the nine planets in the solar system. The 'S' on the Sun is a hint for you to replace the four asterisks with the initial letters of the planets Jupiter, Uranus, Neptune and Earth.

58. Just fill in alternate squares as shown to leave a chessboard and a complete set of chessmen represented by their initial letters.

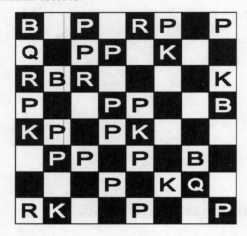

59. **AC**E, TWO, THREE, FOUR, FIVE, SIX, SEVEN, EIGHT, NINE, TEN, **JACK**, **QUEEN**, **K**ING

60. The jewellery is a diamond ring. After the last turn of 45 degrees, the squares on the dial become a ring of diamonds.

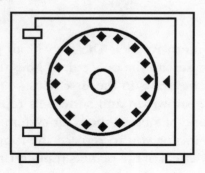

61. baked. Rotate the sequence 90 degrees clockwise and you will see that each word forms a letter in the word FLEECE.

bales canal baled bated level baked

62. He notices that the figures on the clock are Roman numerals.

63. 5 o'clock.

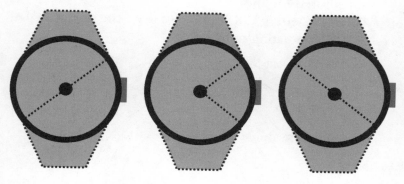

64.

$$\frac{6 \cdot 8}{1 \cdot 7} = 4$$

65. ALL FOR ONE AND ONE FOR ALL. *All* except *for one* of the first four words are repeated in the following well-known phrase.

66. 1. A chimney stack.
     2. A hiding to nothing.
     3. To be seen and not heard.
     4. Go back to square one.
     5. Open and shut case.
     6. Space invader.

67. SUMO. Each letter in the numbers one to six has been substituted for another.

68. Fill in the letters A, R, T and Y to leave the phrase SOLAR SYSTEM radiating outward.

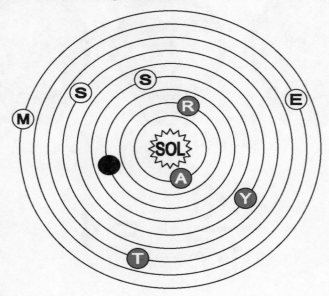

69. ACT. The arrangements of letters and numbers on the left contain the words DODO, ODD and DO.

70. Bristol. **BR** + **I** + **Startstop to Laststop.**

71. Arrange the last five of 'his copper coins' on one side of the TABLE and the first four 'coins' on the other side to get I CONSTABLE COIN, which is one *other* copper coin.

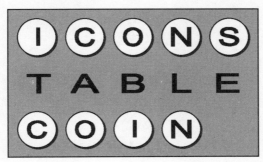

72. Exchange the two xs in 6 x 4 x 25 for two ones (single cubes) to leave the cube number 614125.

73. E to leave the phrase 9 LOZENGES reading from left to right. This is appropriate because the cubes are formed from a total of nine lozenges or rhombi.

74. £9 because the 'wizard leaves the store happy with £1 in his pocket and *a toad*', which sounds like eight owed.

75. END. The first and last letters of each word are repeated four words further down the list with their positions reversed.

SHINE

LICHEN

POSER

DICE

EXODUS

NARWHAL

RAMP

END

76. 20. Lucy actually said that Sarah's not 'a teen'. Emily misheard her.

77. E.

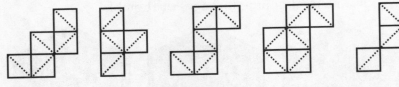

78. Heart attack. HACK outside *new* TATE ART centre.

79. WHAT *is* the missing word. The following words can be read diagonally and upward from left to right: A, AT, AGE, ORE, RAIN, WORST, PHASE, SHAM, BAIT, IF and BE.

80. Viewed from the correct distance % looks like 96 and the equation appears to be $196 + 200 = 396$.

81. Mangetout. The answer is hidden in the man's reply: 'I don't have any, **man. Get out**!'

82. The arrangement now spells aitch in Morse code (taking the boxes as dots and the double boxes as dashes).

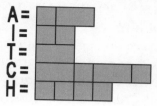

83. 491meters. Substitute the numbers for the appropriate letters to get DIAMETERS.

84. The hands are coincident between the 1 and 2 of 12.

85. Place the King over the right side of the Q on the Queen to leave the letter C. The letters on the last four cards then spell JACK.

86. Coincidentally it is COINCIDENTALLY. This puzzle is simply a cryptic description of this word. COIN+ CIDE(DICE)+N+TALLY.

87 .

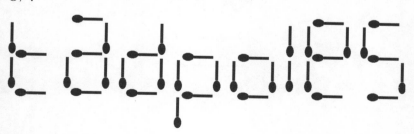

88. dou, which is nop upside-down.
89. Replace the three dots in U.S.A. with the three letters to get SPECTATORS' ROAR HELPS UNSEAT JOCKEY IN KENTUCKY DERBY.
90. Rotate the picture 90 degrees anticlockwise to find 'Los Angeles' when you read downward in the sky.
91. Read down each column of letters to find ISLANDS, TUMBLER and CALCIFY. The missing square contains an L.
92. Because the other missing letters – Q, U, E, S, T, I, O, N, M, A, R and K – are represented by the question mark.
93. VOODOO. The R88 contains the letters in VOODOO.
94. Nothing. They are the two blanks in a set of Scrabble tiles.
95. Add a line to the bottom of the T to form an I and complete 'series' in Morse code.

??? ? ?I? ?? ? ???

96. 27: $3^3 = 27$.
97.

BOTH

RATION

98. Zero. The sum of the lengths of two of the sides of each triangular end is equal to the length of the third side, therefore each end must actually be a straight line and the figure must have no volume because it exists in only two dimensions.

99. The missing letters are F, R, O and M. After all, it does say 'choose from'. The completed words are REFORM, FORUM and ROOMFUL.

100. The sequence of completed letters spells ABRACADABRA.

Creative thinking test 2

The following 20 questions have been designed to test your creative thinking ability. Allow yourself an hour of uninterrupted time to attempt them.

1.   How many ties does Einstein have: seven, eight, nine, ten or eleven?

2.   Can you state the name of the famous building given in this picture?

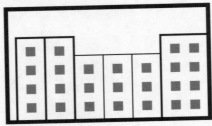

3. A magician places three rabbits numbered 1, 2 and 3 in hat A. Next he puts rabbits 1 and 3 in hat B with the result that 2 does actually disappear from hat A. What is the explanation?

4. Can you see which one of these words is the odd one out?

ACT

CORNY

DICE

ICON

STATIC

5.   Can you find a joker below?

6.   CHAIN is to INGOT as KOYMNCIH GULE is to ?

7.   While on holiday in the United States you notice this sign in the hotel foyer. What does it mean (8, 3, 2 and 5 letters)?

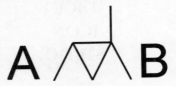

8.   Move two of the six toothpicks below to leave a little sheep going from left to right.

A ⋀⋀ B

9.   What three-letter word can be placed after all three of the following words to create a new word?

CON

FIR

MAT

10. Move one of these planks to leave more than three but less than four.

11. Fill in the missing letters.

_ _ _ _ _<u>F</u>_ _ _ _ _<u>C</u> _ _ _<u>D</u>_ _<u>E</u>_ _ _

12. This is a diagram of the Sun and planets of the solar system. Can you figure out the logic and determine exactly where the Sun and Pluto are?

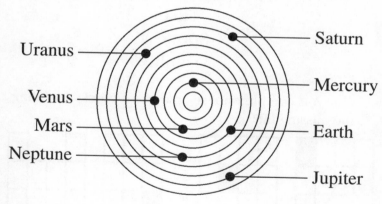

13. What number should replace each question mark in the last two boxes?

7 4 3	4 2 0	0 5 6	0 4 0	? 7 0	0 ? ?
5 0 6	5 5 2	2 0 8	7 4 6	2 0 6	5 3 7
9 2 6	0 9 7	9 4 0	0 5 0	? 3 0	? 0 ?

14. What is the missing number?

1, 13, 16, 61, ?, 217

15. Which one of these words does not belong in this sequence?

Zero

Point

Injustice

Fijian

Spotless

Visibility

16. Can you complete these apartment blocks by filling in the missing lift?

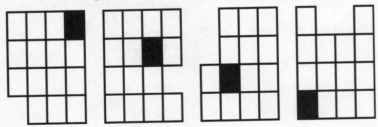

17. What did the Spanish golfer say with an accent at the end of the eighteenth hole?

18. A member of the local chess club frequently uses the other members as a sounding board for her new chess puzzles. Recently she asked them this question: 'Can you find a chess piece containing four letters on this chessboard?'

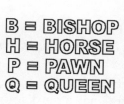

No one at the club could. Can you?

19. Can you work out what the missing letter is?

HEAR IS TO CLOG

BIG IS TO LO

HAIR IS TO ?

20. Can you complete this curious sequence?

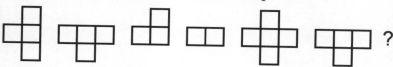

Answers to creative thinking test 2

1. Nine. 'Nine ties' is an anagram of Einstein.
2. Empire State Building. The outlines of the buildings make 'mπr', which sounds like 'empire'.
3. 2 does (female rabbits) disappear from hat A.
4. DICE. In the other words the letter C has a hard sound.
5. J (Jack) + 0 (Nothing) + K (King) + ER (Queen).
6. QUESTION MARK. Shift each letter forward six positions in the alphabet.
7. Elevator out of order.
8.

9. ION. CON-FIR-MAT-ION.

10. The spaces between the planks form pi, which is approximately equal to 3.14.

11. The number of lines in each group of lines beneath each letter corresponds with the position of that letter in the alphabet. The letters spell FACADE.

_ _ _ _ **F**_ **A** _ _**C A** _ _**D**_ _**E**_ _ _

12. The circles represent the Sun and the planets and their relative sizes. The Sun and Pluto are therefore represented by the largest and smallest circles respectively.

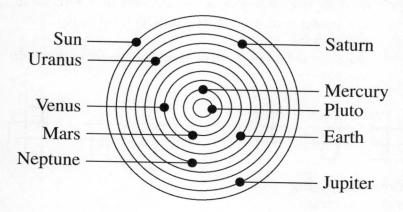

13. The zeroes correspond with the positions of the spots on each side of a die, so each question mark should be replaced with a zero.

14. 128. The differences between the numbers in the series are 12, 3, 45, 67 and 89.

15. Spotless. Each successive word in the sequence contains an extra spot.

16. Add the letters in LIFT as follows to complete the apartment buildings:

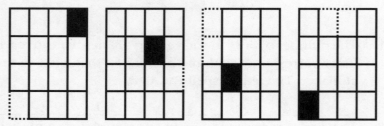

17. Olé because it is at the end of the eighteenth h-ole.

18. HHPP because it sounds like 'a chess piece'.

19. N. Each line of letters is an anagram of a profession. The professions are ARCHEOLOGIST, BIOLOGIST and HISTORIAN.

20. The lines inside each shape form the letters in the word curious.

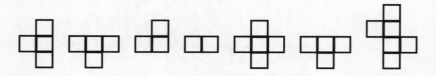

Creativity rating

1–5	Average
6–10	Above average
11–15	Very creative
16–20	Extremely creative

Further reading from Kogan Page

Other titles in the testing series

Career, Aptitude and Selection Tests, Jim Barrett, 1998

How to Master Personality Questionnaires, 2nd edn, Mark Parkinson, 2000

How to Master Psychometric Tests, 2nd edn, Mark Parkinson, 2000

How to Pass Advanced Aptitude Tests, Jim Barrett, 2002

How to Pass Advanced Numeracy Tests, Mike Byron, 2002

How to Succeed at an Assessment Centre, Harry Tolley and Bob Wood, 2001

How to Pass Computer Selection Tests, Sanjay Modha, 1994

How to Pass Graduate Psychometric Tests, 2nd edn, Mike Bryon, 2001

How to Pass Numeracy Tests, 2nd edn, Harry Tolley and Ken Thomas, 2000

How to Pass Numerical Reasoning Tests, Heidi Smith, 2003

How to Pass Professional-level Psychometric Tests, Sam Al-Jajjoka, 2001

How to Pass Selection Tests, 2nd edn, Mike Bryon and Sanjay Modha, 1998

How to Pass Technical Selection Tests, Mike Bryon and Sanjay Modha, 1993

How to Pass the Civil Service Qualifying Tests, 2nd edn Mike Bryon, 2003

How to Pass the Police Initial Recruitment Test, Harry Tolley, Ken Thomas and Catherine Tolley, 1997

How to Pass Verbal Reasoning Tests, 2nd edn Harry Tolley and Ken Thomas, 2000

Rate Yourself!, Marthe Sansregret and Dyane Adams, 1998

Test Your Emotional Intelligence, Bob Wood and Harry Tolley, 2002

Test Your IQ, Ken Russell and Philip Carter, 2000

Test Your Own Aptitude, 3rd edn, Jim Barrett and Geoff Williams, 2003

Test Yourself!, Jim Barrett, 2000

The Times Book of IQ Tests–Book Three, Ken Russell and Philip Carter, 2003

The Times Book of IQ Tests–Book Two, Ken Russell and Philip Carter, 2002

The Times Book of IQ Tests–Book One, Ken Russell and Philip Carter, 2001

Also available on CD ROM in association with *The Times*

Published by Kogan Page Interactive, *The Times* Testing Series is an exciting new range of interactive CD ROMs that will provide invaluable, practice tests for both job applicants and for those seeking a brain-stretching challenge. Each CD ROM features:

- over 1,000 unique interactive questions;
- instant scoring with feedback and analysis;
- hours of practice with randomly generated test;
- questions devised by top UK MENSA puzzles editors and test experts;
- against-the-clock, real test conditions.

Current titles available:
> *Brain Teasers Volume 1*, 2002
> *Psychometric Tests Volume 1*, 2002
> *Test Your IQ Volume 1*, 2002
> *Test Your Aptitude Volume 1*, 2002

Interview and career guidance

The A–Z of Careers and Jobs, 10th edn, Irene Krechowiecka, 2002

Act Your Way Into a New Job, Deb Gottesman and Buzz Mauro, 1999

Changing Your Career, Sally Longson, 2000

Choosing Your Career, Simon Kent, 1997

Creating Your Career, Simon Kent, 1997

From CV to Shortlist, Tony Vickers, 1997

Graduate Job Hunting Guide, Mark Parkinson, 2001

Great Answers to Tough Interview Questions, 5th edn, Martin John Yate, 2001

How You Can Get That Job!, 3rd edn, Rebecca Corfield, 2003

The Job-Hunters Handbook, 2nd edn, David Greenwood, 1999

Job-Hunting Made Easy, 3rd edn, John Bramham and David Cox, 1995

Landing Your First Job, Andrea Shavick, 1999

Net That Job!, 2nd edn, Irene Krechowiecka, 2000

Odd Jobs, 2nd edn, Simon Kent, 2002

Offbeat Careers, 3rd edn, Vivien Donald, 1995

Online Job-Hunting: Great Answers to Tough Interview Questions, Martin John Yate and Terra Dourlain, 2001

Preparing Your Own CV, 3rd edn, Rebecca Corfield, 2003

Readymade CVs, 2nd edn, Lynn Williams, 2000

Readymade Job Search Letters, 2nd edn, Lynn Williams, 2000

Successful Interview Skills, 3rd edn, Rebecca Corfield, 2002
Your Job Search Made Easy, 3rd edn, Mark Parkinson, 2002

Further advice on a variety of specific career paths can also be found in Kogan Page's *Careers in ...* series and *Getting a Top Job in ...* series. Please visit the Web site at the address below for more details.

The above titles are available from all good bookshops. For further information, please contact the publisher at the following address:

Kogan Page Limited
120 Pentonville Road
London N1 9JN
Tel: 020 7278 0433
Fax: 020 7837 6348
www.kogan-page.co.uk

You can find more of Lloyd's fun puzzle creations at his Web sites iQED!, VINCI and ISI-S:

iQED!
http://homepage.ntlworld.com/atalanta/index.html

VINCI
http://homepage.ntlworld.com/atalanta/vinci/index.html

ISI-S
http://homepage.ntlworld.com/atalanta/isi-s/index.html